THE
WOUNDS
BETWEEN
OUR
STARS

THE
WOUNDS
BETWEEN
OUR
STARS

POEMS BY

TICHINA
WARD-PRATT

The Wounds Between Our Stars
© 2024 Tichina Ward-Pratt
ISBN: 979-8-218-42590-6

First Edition, 2024

Printed in the United States of America

Edited by Laura Joy Phillips
Cover Design by Kim Gaeta
Layout Design by Amy Garbin

for my family and hometown

'scuse me while I kiss the sky
-Jimi Hendrix

you don't know me like the sun, you've never seen my horizon
-Noname

CONTENTS

JUPITER III

NEPTUNE IV

THE WOUNDS BETWEEN OUR STARS

VENUS

I

Venus has a thick atmosphere, traps heat, and
is the hottest planet in our solar system.

The Moon and I

Sometimes I stare at the moon
right outside my window
like it came to visit me,
tell me about its day;
about how much sun it got
and its plan of one day being a star;
of being bright enough,
or big enough
for something to orbit it.
We have this in common,
the moon and I.

Testing 1 2 3

Can you hear me?
I teach mathematics
to a room
of microphones
when yelling
you still can't hear
Speakers distorted, vocals unclear

Testing
1
       2
           3
My kids are machines
Sitting in front of screens
typing the answers
to a failed dream

No one's listening to the static
on the ground
or between their fingers
and the keys
When they dare
to amplify their voices
they are still deceived

We think we are teaching them
But they are teaching us
just how useless stars can be
when they don't shine bright enough

How many hundreds of years
will it take to notice their light
To click to station 123.4
Testing if you're still listening?

The district assesses students day after day
Simplify the following expression.
click
Solve the equation.
click
How many total students?
click
What is x?
click

Click
Click
Until they are the bait
used to catch
the biggest fish
the biggest profit
Until they are profitable

Testing
1
      2
        3
Are you listening?
How many tests will it take
before our education system fails?
Before we realize
how ill-prepared we are
on a global scale

Our students
prepared to work
but not to lead
Complying,
hands up
then hands down
on the keys

Testing 123 times
and counting
counting to stay alive
counting to stay a lie
counting because
we tell them it's
the only thing
they have

Test 1: sit down
Test 2: be quiet
Test 3: sit still
Which one will they fail?
1
       2
             All?
Careful they end up
in a prison cell
trusting a system that believed
a test could liberate them

Some People Have Courage

I think I'm gonna head out...
but what I really mean is
time to exit before you notice
or start to question my intentions
to be with you,
to stare in your eyes,
to watch your skin as you wake
and fall asleep.

I'm getting really tired...
but what I really mean is,
are you tired of me yet?
Is it too much that I want to
sit in your presence?
Does the silence scare you;
make you think that
there is something more?
Maybe it's just me;

                    Maybe it's just me

                                    Maybe it's just me

It is just me;
afraid of how foolish I'll look
when you see me exposed:
red white and bone.
You'll laugh,
thinking my desire was pathological
like the devil asking God
to give him the world.

I have to get up really early...
but I'd rather it be next to you.
As we plan out our days together,
tell me about your dreams.
Not just your aspirations,
but where your mind went
as you slept. Where do you keep
your heart—locked away,
on your front doorstep,
behind the passenger seat
in your car?
I'm not afraid of a scavenger hunt.
I'm afraid that you will eventually see me.

It's getting really late...
But what I really mean is I'm afraid
because I do not yet see myself
and it seems selfish
to ask for your hand on this journey.
Maybe I have courage
the way some people have faith:
that of a mustard seed.

Black Is Incredibly Vast

I hate you, because I hate myself.
You lied to me when you told me that my skin
was blacker than the charcoal that burned
under the grill on the 4th of July;
my skin was darker than the night sky
accented by the fire works;
my blood was the evil in you,
one over thirty-two; my lips were too big,
too fat, too wide, must hide behind my hurt.

But fuck all that. Put it on a plate and display it
to the world, because if we
are the ones that held you up,
then you are the ones
who will fall if we let you go.

Black is beautiful
Black is beautiful
Black is a battle in me

If I were to see myself,
then I would see them.
I don't see them.
You don't see them.
Freddie Gray, Miriam Carey,
Tony Robinson, Tanisha Anderson,
Malissa Williams, Timothy Russell,
Yvette Smith, we didn't see them.

They were caught
between los intersticios;
These two worlds
were at odds with them.
They didn't fit in one;
they fit in both.

Black is part
Black is whole
Black is a veil

We are the heavens
and the earth, Venus and Mars.
You are our Cupid filled with lust
and desire for erotic love,
mesmerized by the sky
between the stars,
mesmerized by the sun
between the planets of our hearts.
That sun is the hurt, the pain, the sorrow,
the negro spirituals borrowed
from womb of darkness,
the fuel that will spark this revolution.

Black is revolution
Black is retribution
Black is

Uncover your mask
and over-masculine ways.
We can kill the daze with our beauty,
hide the sun with our unity,
take over the world with our mutiny.
This Black beauty, see, is incredibly vast;
cast the first stone if you
don't want to see us pass.
But when we duck you jeopardize
your own glass house.

We've created liberty in the forms
of our sorrow songs and taken
truth spoken through the mouths
of Black youth through poetry; dance along

cause Black is flower
Black is power
Black is

Accommodating Comet

Your mind, like butterflies
trapped in a black painted jar:
colorful and dark
free and confined
loud and muffled
but I loved them

Once so in love
I gave you an invitation
Once so in love
I stopped because it hurt
Like sit-ups to the sun
Irrational

Like I've memorized 78 digits of pi
Why? I don't know;
the same reasons for loving you,
Irrational

Like traveling to the sun
Just to see how hot
Just to see how far I could go
Irrational

Like sit-ups to the sun
Now my abs hurt
and sometimes the scars
make me unrecognizable
I couldn't reach far enough
I'm sorry I was so ambitious
I understood so much about your hurt
that it blinded me from my own

I, an accommodating comet,
that could only destroy itself,
crashed into the sun and evaporated
I was just a sungazer
and you were the sun
Vain enough to let me burn

A Butcher's Wet Dream

If you made one thousand
precise cuts upon my chest,
you still wouldn't find my heart.

It's hidden in the book
"Avoiding Vulnerability for Dummies."
It be bobbin' and weavin' like Ali,
but still afraid of the dark
like my 2-year-old cousin.

Afraid to be punctured,
opened, exposed, broken.
Pick any knife if you will;
my veins be made of steel.

My blood still like water,
but mighty like the ocean.
Cut til you tired. Cut til you kill.
I don't need to heal.
A butcher's wet dream.

Trying to Repair Ceramic Pots

My eyes heavy, filled with cement
by my ex-lover who I left to love myself.
An attempt to recall forgotten memories,
when this pain was energy
but that fire inside of me
was never bright; it was just hot.
And you were never bold; you just drank.

You said we would grow old; now we not.
But I feared wrinkled skin
and gray hairs, like you feared love.
We were at opposite sides of the water and
our messages never made it
to the other side of the ocean.
The bottles had too many holes in them.

We were broken, so broken
that we couldn't recognize smooth clay anymore;
our ceramics were always in pieces.
They were so small, we gave up trying
to put them back together and they
deformed with the change of the weather.
How did we get here?

I've never seen pain, misery, headaches,
and tears so often under fragmented skies.
Fog covered the stars that we could
no longer see ourselves reflected in.
But we were no stars.
We thought we could radiate
through the clouds but then it rained.
It poured.
It hailed.
We failed.

Vinyl Vinyl Vinyl

Let me be happy
I had to tell myself

Let me be happy
I had to tell myself

I took my soul out of the garage
and placed it on the record player
I listened to the surface
noise of my own heart
and waited for only one track

I almost forced myself
to listen to the others
I wasn't in the mood;
lifted the tonearm
regret skip; fear skip

I flipped the record
lowered the tonearm
and gently dropped the stylus
I waited to acknowledge
my own happiness

I waited to acknowledge
my own happiness

The track skipped
Repeat; my anxiety rose an octave
I listened again
It was me alive on vinyl

It was me alive on vinyl
It was me alive on vinyl

Lucid Barley

I have an obsession with spirits.
They call my name
ever so sweet,
tart, neat, balanced.

We stand at the crossroads
on tightrope and fall into place.
Taste the bitters
on their luminescent tongue,
numb but ever so sweet
like malted barley.

I smell red apple on their breath,
oak, and notes of sugar maple
transcending into the sun-shaded trees.

You've Been Exposed

To be vulnerable,
even a little bit,
is like an exposition;
a display of every
emotion I've ever felt
with a tragic ending of death
where only I knew
I wasn't a martyr,
just a coward too afraid
to be revealed.

Not a Stupid Question

I was once asked if I ever
considered plastic surgery.
I said, *Nah*. I'll just try to radically
love myself and loudly force the sun
to look gracefully at the moon.

I smile while my left breast ridicules
the right for not being big enough;
chastises it for not being average,
not fitting in, not taking up space,
not being enough.
A love like sibling rivalry.

My body always attacking itself
and the scars still a victory
of a battle within, a victory
that I hang on my wall as a reminder
that I have triumphed. I have allowed
my body to shelter me from the storm.
I am not afraid to sit with my thoughts
and allow them to fight psychological warfare.

In My Silence: The Mask that Almost Became My Face

When I take off my mask,
all 59 pounds of it,
sometimes it leaves scars around my temple.

They heal fast on a good day.
On a good day, I am proud of myself
for taking a leap of faith.
On a bad day, I am angry
that I allowed myself to fall for so long.

My back toward the ground,
unable to predict when I would hit.
If I could hit, how hard would the impact be?

Would my bones recover?
Would my doctor prescribe the right medication?
Anxiety kicks in like gravity
as I try to find a part of the mountain
close enough to me, protruding just enough
to latch onto before my ultimate demise.

On a good day, my bones recover
in a way that's stronger than before.
On a bad day, I latch onto the side
of the mountain and hold on for dear life.

23

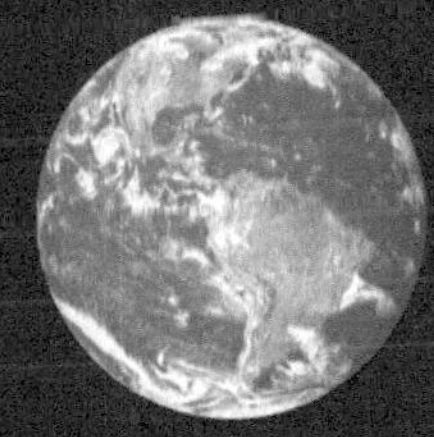

EARTH

II

Earth is the only planet in our solar system that supports life.

Fibroids

Day -30: faulty vagina
He asked me what was wrong with me.
As if I could see all of my flaws.
A fool who believed that sex was easy.
Not complex in its intentions to make me unusable.
I thought that maybe I should return it
for all its bad press. Doctors and gynecologists
interviewing me at the stake. A *witch*
that couldn't please, they said.
A vagina that didn't need, they said.

//

Day -7: deadly alive
Cut me open already.
Remove this tumor.
Leave me exposed,
unconscious.
Exsanguinate my anxiety.
Let it seep from my pores
and stain the ground,
so that I can walk past this
crimson concrete and know
that I had just enough blood
to keep me alive.

//

Day 1: bobby pins
You can't have any bobby pins
in your hair is all I could remember
from being in the prep room.
That and how she didn't really look at me.
I took them out, walked through the door
leading to the waiting room,
and handed them to my mother.
I would see her 4 days later, wishing
I had those bobby pins to hold me;
hold me together.

//

Day 1.5: five days
Covid guidelines prohibited
company after surgery.
No visitors for five days.
No squeezes from Mom
to comfort my bruised soul.
No stern voice from Dad
ensuring they put each
puzzle piece in the right spot.

//

Day 2: ten staples

A sudden movement brought pain,
like I was split in half and my other
half had gotten away from me.
There were more than
ten staples holding me together.
I can't remember how they knew
that I didn't have enough
blood to stain the ground.

//

Day 3: unfinished puzzle

She exposed my body.
The amount of drugs in my system
overpowered my dignity.
I was too ashamed to tell her
to put my puzzle back together.
She was more concerned
with her wasted time and didn't believe me
when I told her that one of the pieces
was not in the right spot.
Who was I to know my own pain?
If I could see how this moment
would change me forever, I would've mustered
just enough courage to tightly close my gown
and iron over each piece
so they could never come undone.

//

Day 4: broken levee

They scanned my butchered parts
to identify the one responsible.
They found him still holding on
after the bad parts were removed.
The doctor told me that
I was not allowed to eat.
Complications, my stomach
was filled with blood.
The culprit, a broken levee.
I didn't want to be cut open again.

//

Day 7: pillows

My parents bought me ten pillows,
maybe one for each staple.
My little apartment was a palace,
compared to cold floors and loud hallways.
I cherished it even more now;
the privacy, the control, the comfort.

Betwixt and Between

Dreaming,
underneath the rivers
that drain on the 28th day.
Following the moon,
I fell through
consumed by the current
betwixt the dual forces of
masculine and feminine.
Small,
whirling,
controlled by the parents
of still opinion.
Unable to escape the night
or release the waters
from the frozen mountains.
Fountains of joy silenced
and thrown into poor.
Yet I stand, unexpressive
still, my heart locked
within the womb.

Same Smile

You were just like me
Same smile
Same laugh
Same smile
Damn that smile

We didn't even know each other.
Yet our teachers knew we were
gonna succeed when we grew up.
You had a way of making people feel
comfortable around you.
Never had no downs only ups.
They called us tough
cause we played basketball,
but we weren't too tall.
We were good enough to get around
everyone and shoot the ball.

There was that one hall they named after you
cause you were so popular your shoes
left permanent footprints on the wall.
And they say magic isn't real.
But you don't know how it feels
to not share the sunlight with you.

Our paths never crossed,
but left the same marks.
Our voices never aligned,
but our minds were so intertwined.
Our goals connected, but our souls
were rejected to two different worlds.

After unnamed gunshots splatte-te-te-tered
like firecrackers heard loud from around the corner,
your soul became supernatural.
Our pitch was less equilateral and
the underworld held our song as collateral.

We were no longer we
just you and me.
Completely different.
The verses of our songs illiterate as the wind
erased our words from memory

I was just like you
Same smile
Same laugh
Same smile
Damn that smile

To the Boy Who Spends His Afternoons in the Bookstore off of Spring Street, I Swear to God I'm Not a Stalker

After Rudy Francisco
"The Girl Who Works at Starbucks, Down the Street from My House on Del Mar Heights Road, I Swear to God I'm Not a Stalker"

When I asked you if you knew
where the poetry section was,
I really meant to say, *I overheard a conversation.*
I turned my head slightly and had to know
if your voice was as beautiful as your smile.

Instead I got nervous, asked a question
I already knew the answer to.
Had passed the poetry aisle twice,

even sat down for that matter.

I imagine that when God made you,
she gazed for the first time.
Turned to an angel, gave him dap
and said *He's gone be a killer.*
You're that gorgeous.

I spent the next few days wondering
how I would introduce myself to you properly.
I think I figured it out.
It's gonna be something like, *Hey.*

That's what I've come up with so far,
but I think I'm getting somewhere.

Lost in the Light

That summer was cold and suffocating
You had made another mistake
our father did not forgive
I cried for you

We didn't see it coming
We were confused by a story,
that outsiders ran with, painted
on your chest, and forced down your throat
Now you're starving cause you have yet to swallow
The hole in your heart had made the surface hollow

I fear someone would pierce it and erase
the little bit of life you had left
I cried for you
Wondered what you did to pass the time
Did our mother, find it difficult
to see you caged like an animal, too wild to be let loose

Did she humanize you so that your soul could lift
from the soles of your feet and welcome her
into the vacancy you no longer lived

I don't know if my letter was enough
to serve as a mental break for your sanity
A warmness to the cold summer
A window to a steam room of mosquitoes
trying to drain your blood
A picture in the middle of a chapter book
overlooking the ocean

I don't know if my letter was enough
to reach a boy who lost himself on the way
to the light that burned you with flying fists from father
and lone doorsteps from mother

I remember the sounds you made
Like the air from your lungs was being beaten
out of your mouth for the greater good
Now the sound is imprisoned inside my lungs
so they can remember the day they gave up on you

Sleeping on a Full Brain

10:30pm Bed Tiiiiiiime. But what if I move back to Oakland? Rent has gone up. What about my life in LA? All my friends. Bitch you ain't got no friends. I'll have to start over. Back to square one. Damn. Well you'll have your family. My mama gone try to make me go to church every Sunday. The hell I am. Jesus forgive me. Teachers probably get paid more in The Bay anyway. LAUSD ain't shit. Let me not try my karma fo' they lay my ass off. My mama gone have me running errands and shit. Younger sibling gone be asking me for money. Damn. That's why they phone turned off. Well it would feel good to help out. Help my mom clean up around the house. I mean I could put like 40 miles between us instead of 359 miles.

11:00pm Damn I should take my ass to sleep. Where I put that fuckin paper I was supposed to take to Kaiser. Now I gotta go and look through all them papers. Damn it's 2020 nigga, y'all motherfuckahs can't use encrypted emails. Well, I was the one that misplaced that shit. *sigh* Did I renew my driver's license? Shit. Is that shit due today? Fuck I gotta get my ass up. You know what that shit due next month on the 5th. I just looked at that shit. Damn. Maybe I'm losing my memory cause I'm not sleeping well. Nigga that ain't a thing.

11:30pm Let me go to the bathroom then go to sleep. Did that bitch give me my $20 back? Damn. Stop giving people money you ain't Santa Claus nigga or the motherfuckin bank. She was supposed to return that book I lent her too. Talking bout I'll send it when I find it. You the one that reached out to me nigga. How you gone send me some shit you can't find. All kinds of backwards. You generous ass motherfuckah.

12:00am Let me just say the alphabet backwards. Z.... Y.... X.... damn what comes before X. ehh. That lying ass nigga. Talking about we can go anywhere I choose. If we can go anywhere then why we can't go to the four places I already suggested to yo ass. Then that nigga just gone bail. Talking about he had an appointment. What appointment you made that you didn't know you had in advance. Just tell the truth, you lying ass nigga.

12:30am *yawn* Is it 12:30? Damn. Did I put them clothes in the dryer? I hope it doesn't get mildew. I could get up and see. I'm so comfortable though. It'll probably be good til the morning.

People Begin to Think Differently
When the Danger Ends

S h e
hit the ground
with fear in her belly.
Life was never predictable in
a war zone. Bullets flew like they
owned the air, and they could
take it from your lips if you were
foolish   enough. Hide, for only bullets kill
bullets. He walked right past the door she was behind; a nail
shop where the owner changed the sign on the door to closed.
He read it and knew death better than Lucifer, because he had
fallen too and she was just a cloud he passed on his way down. He would
fall through one or two; separate them into pieces and never look back.
They were collateral damage and so was she. He shot a man, a cop, and then
they shot him. But when the danger all ends, she is safe; home.

GO PEE!

*Announcement: Student have to wait for an administrator
to escort them to the restroom due to the increased
number of fights happening around the school.*

Solution: punish all students, assume they're all
susceptible to violence by way of the bathroom.

Reality: *The stress involved in holding
your pee is not important to me.*

*I don't trust you.
You're incapable;
All students are the same.
All students are destructive.*

I could go on and on and on about how schools
are no longer a means to education, how love
is no longer a means to discovery and revelation, and
how we teach our students to hold their breath.

What are they supposed to do,
when we always tell them don't?
Don't speak, don't chew, don't pee, don't move.
Why come to school when they can't
even be trusted to go to the fucking bathroom?
THIS IS NOT A PRISON!

They are musicians and the world is their instrument.
Let them blow like Coltrane,
feel the air come up from their diaphragm,
and inhale deeply because they fucking can!
Go Pee!
Sometimes it's their only opportunity to release.

Between the World and Me

*"And what did it mean that number two pencils, conjugations without context,
Pythagorean theorems, handshakes, and head nods were the difference between
life and death, were the curtains drawing down between the world and me"*

—Ta-Nehisi Coates

What is significant to you is a matter of life and death for us
You use handshakes to close interviews
We use them to close deals

March 27th, 2010, Eric Toscano was fatally shot in the head at his birthday
party up the street from my house
He was only 18
With plans to play college football at Chico State
The 17-year-old boy who pulled the trigger was rejected at the door and
came back shooting

Every bullet made an innocent guilty and put a price on this face
In 17 years he was like a vase:
drop him on the floor and his masculinity would break
Learn to react first
then to be quiet...
Bury your emotions until they retire
With enough in their 401(k) to never work again

You see, you use head nods to initiate conversations
We use them to initiate treaties that silence wars ongoing since the begin-
ning of this nation
Call us Malcolm X; We are fighting the enemy but deep down we want
peace

August 11th, 2015, Caylen Gooch's body was found lying in the street after
being shot to death by a 20 year old in Mableton, Georgia
He was only 19
In his second year at Clayton State University
My aunt moved them out there to escape the violent streets of Oakland
You see, the difference between life and death is accepting the things you
cannot change

Two worlds, in an attempt to overlap created a contradiction not an eclipse
that conflate the significant with the insignificant
Cuz respect never held so much weight
And time was never a safe haven for fate

You see, you use number two pencils to write freely
We use them to free the thoughts in our minds
Detach the evil spirits like strange fruit whose rinds get left behind

Winter 2011 Matt lied to our father about why he was running from the
Bart station
He was in a hurry to get home,
but later told me that two men nearly killed him for his wallet
He pushed one into the other and ran for his life
I guess when you're a track star, you think you're invincible

*Maybe the difference between life and death is not accepting the things that you
cannot change
But changing the things that you cannot accept*

Cranberry Juice

I see your face in the depths of the shadows.
Mind constructing your piercing eyes,
daring curves, trigonometric curls
just as I remember it:

morphing together with fan fashioned fantasies
of your lips on mine, your body
on mine, your house or mine.

Blinded by the possibility of death and freedom.
Dead possibilities of your hands
tracing the outer edges of my skeleton.
Free of anxiety, free anxiety,
freedom or anxiety from the tug of war;
the pull of could've beens and
the push of should've beens.

Both a kind of closure.
Close her back up
or undress her consented.
Contentedly, I rave in passion
fruit we can cash in
from the production of our magic.

Cranberry juice on the inside of my cheek;
tart,
sweet,
crimson,
like blood love letters written in bitten tongues.

You Thought

You said *World?*

                                        The World said *huh?*

You said *Revolve around me.*

Before it could answer,

        you
            walked
                away
                    believing
                        it
                          would
                            follow
                              you.

A Love Letter to Oakland

You introduced me to the dew in the mornings;
the paint that confessed its comfort in the arms of the bridges,
walls, and the sides of Bart trains;
the Nike's hanging from telephone wires;
of beauty, hope, and dreams
So much so that it was magic
that I embraced like birthday cake, a mouthful

But if I truly believed in magic,
then maybe the 16 bullets that pierced my uncle's body
would have stopped in midair and fallen to the ground
as he assumed the power of Magneto in X men

Or that the gun pulled out on my younger brother
by two hooded men was filled with water
and they were all starring in their own movie
called Super Soakers in the Hood

Or the prison my older brother was locked away in
was in fact a secret base to organize human existence
on Mars and they needed all the time they could get

I can't afford to believe that you could show me the world
and then set it on fire, but then try to convince me
that it was rain replenishing the land,
that I could just ignore death like photosynthesis

JUPITER
III

Jupiter is like a star, but never gets big enough to start burning.

A Birthday Eulogy

Saturn has returned
to the position it once was
at the time of my birth.
I'm waiting at 29's doorstep,
wondering how
I'm pushing 30.

The number of cousins
I've seen in caskets,
the number of siblings
I've seen in chains,
made me believe that
Oakland children
weren't meant to age.

The grave I dug myself
now trying to smooth
with cement and water.

My new occupation,
a concrete mixer trying to
make up for lost holes.
Every funeral
a piece of my heart.

But don't ask me to speak;
I might choke
on my own healing
that lodged itself into my throat
hoping to make a voice
out of my trachea.

I refuse to shout
as if my life is more precious
than those taken
from their mothers.

her screams I remember
her pain I remember
her face I remember

A stain on my soul
that I never thought
I would outlive.

Yet here I am alive
and breathing
and hoping that
death doesn't kill me.

Your Smile Wide, Like Watermelon

Bright like when the sun used the ocean
as a mirror after rising in the morning

Your smile crooked, like it knew perfection
was overrated; a scam at best
The fine print on a prescription bottle
that included everything but death

Your smile small, like ignore obvious big and
too elaborate to hold truth

Your smile silent, like an inside joke
between your eyes and your cheeks
Read like a single sentence on a page;
the space loud enough for everyone to hear

Your smile enough; serve it on a platter
Read it on a menu with no words

307 Miles North

It was San Francisco spring when I got the news. I was on the train with good company, friends and sunkissed windows. I had no words for how I felt. Before this moment, I was hopeless but somehow found it in me to pray. Maybe this was God showing me just how amazing she could be. I was accepted to the college of my dreams and my father's face said it all. The last time that I had seen him cry was at Grandma's funeral. But how could this be my greatest accomplishment? Since stepping onto this campus, I missed my family every nightfall. It was fall and I was falling into a deep depression. Signs of struggle were so prevalent amongst us all that no one knew I needed saving. I was nearly dismissed and I needed a fix, an assist, of any kind but my eyes were blinded by what my ignorant professor had said to me. He made some remarks about where I was from. Somehow my concerns were negligible. My home, Oakland, had prepared me enough to fend for myself. I had to get an A in that class was all I thought of. Subject-to-dismissal was more than a warning, it was returning the torch to my ancestors' grave and allowing it to catch fire. I did not have enough energy to be angry. I just wanted it all to end, but I remember that look on my father's face and thought of college nearly skipping yet another generation. This was not my intention, but everyone else was 307 miles north and I was here, waiting for God to show me just how amazing she could be.

In My Loud: The Legacy No One Told Me About

I planted a seed in a desert storm
and the sand scratched away at my skin
You could see the red, white,
and pink as I got closer to the ground
in which this seed was to grow

I grew it with the tears I shed from the pain
The crimson scars were the outer layers
of the onion that needed to be peeled
and discarded so that my senses
could embrace just how potent
the core could be

The skin I shed covered the hole
I never told anyone that the seed
came from my stomach
It was too dark to grow there

The seed eventually grew so tall
that it attracted the masses
My body didn't make it
They called the event, the rebirth

Deadly Promise

I take advantage of all
the space you hold:
using it for storage,
and worries, and doubt
I panic when you get too full

You expand like if I open my mouth
I would vomit out my anxiety
Chest so fragile
Lungs not used to capacity
until I'm forced to breathe deeply
I recall my mistakes and
promise never to misuse you again

I know you hurt like I do
I feel it too
The troubles that I hold
are not accustomed
to my body: oversized
I should have read the tags

Give me another chance
to make it right
I have learned from
my near-deadly mistakes
and hope you still have some room
for me to exhale fully

Crawling Monsters

I wonder why my fears so Benjamin Button—
getting younger as I get older,
yet to be outgrown.
When I came out to my mother,
I could feel the monsters crawling
from under my bed, relieved
that after all this time,
I could see that they were real.

When my younger sibling came out,
Mom said that she could see a weight
lift from their shoulders, like they
had been carrying their greatest fear
and now it had vanished.

For me, it felt like nothing was going to get easier.
I would lay down on my bed
while the monsters tear away at my flesh
piece by piece.

Forced Soliloquy

My mind is another being.
I ask it questions,
and it responds
clear as the sky after rainfall,
empathetic like it cradled my heart
to sleep on a restless night,
real like it could see the thoughts
I kept hidden from the world.

Sometimes wrong and deceiving.
Why did it make me lose
control of my face? Make my eyes imagine
something that wasn't there?
Why did it ease pain in a troubled moment
regardless of outsider stares?
Their eyebrows raising ever so slightly,
confused at the time I'm having,
alone with my thoughts.

The Divide

The huge line, the cut, the divide
As you take the rapid down, the trees
slowly fade away as if poverty
was underneath the wealth of the day
Like a hidden treasure that one's
eyes might glance over for a taste of the sunset
that seemed a little golder

Cold nights sometimes it rains
but it floods in poverty's pain
Our emotions drained to the sewers
with the hopes of a sky bluer
As the evil in our faces turn into representations,
we are the marked souls of an evil nation
The huge line, the cut, the divide

Terrifying hills that cast their shadow
upon us, use our toil as trophies
and plant their leeches on our necks;
sucking the blood from the lambs
like vampire imperialist

It was cutthroat, cut throats
and watch the blood drizzle
over the body like icing on cake
Can't begin to make sense
We are senseless beings in tight dresses
that are tearing at the seams
The huge line, the cut, the divide

So deep we are trapped between
the edges of our own epidermis
that was supposed to keep us warmer
but instead kept us hurting
So wide, sometimes we all fall through
in the comfort of our own ignorance
Claiming belligerence
The huge line, the cut, the divide

Intergenerational Trauma

1.   Great Grandmother was beaten
by white nationalists on her walk home
from the grocery store.
Her face, the bruised tomato that fell
and rolled away from the bunch;
alone, but still rolling
from the momentum of the hill.
She died when I was a baby.
Still the story haunts me
like a vacant house with no lights.

2.   Grandmother left her child in the car
and entered her home to a drug raid.
she too, was left in a car but
shackled and separated from the world.

3.   Mother was jumped but not alone,
initiated by her own.
A gang made blankets
out of cracked concrete.
Now, her pain found a home.
A story she could only tell me in passing.

4.   Home was no longer home now
      that Pain enlisted into the army.
      Pregnant,
      bears child,
      no longer enlisted.

5.   Love ruined and left a stain;
      father cheated and left a hole
      that I can still see the bottom of.
      Mother bears again.

6.   A Newborn; a Poet
      from ruin and stain,
      from vacant house with no lights,
      from emptiness from shame,
      alone again.

Not a Bad Listener

I listen without interruption
to the way you drag the last word
between your sentences
when you've nearly lost your train of thought.

I listen until it arrives at the station,
until your eyes roll back down
and around like the wheels on the track;
until they meet the corner of your mouth;
a smile; a choo chooooo:
The idea has a home.

I listen to the pauses;
the clouds making space between your words;
a cushion; a couch
I sit on and rest and wait.

I listen without interruption
to the butterflies flapping loudly in your head,
making it hard for you to connect the dots.
I wait for the links to be made,
for a spider to slowly create a web so strong
I could ride it like a rollercoaster,
making stops at every vertex.
I listen to you without interruption.

Foxy Shirley

I see you
snapping, swaying to the soulful
sounds of Al Green.
I feel a warmth,
a pillow of foam,
a meadow of fox hair.
Looking directly into my enamored eyes
you say,
What you know about that?
As you laugh the sun to the west, I awake.
Ginger inhabits my tongue,
closes all doors and locks itself in,
resting alongside my tastebuds;
exposing the stars hidden
amongst the midnight blue.

*Cocktail Recipe:</u>
Foxy Shirley

Grenadine 1oz
Spicy Ginger Syrup 0.25oz
Fresh Lemon Juice 1oz
Aquafaba 1oz
Sparkling Water 3oz

Prayers to the Sun

My dad loves astronomy.
He can go on and on about warp speed,
how big Jupiter is,
and the asteroid belt.

He once told me, *You know they say*
we could only last 15 seconds in space.
It's cold and there's no oxygen or gravity.
That's what's gonna get you first, he said.
It's all just darkness.

I wondered why that fascinated me so much:
the darkness then sudden death,
the decompression then expansion,
the vacuum then immediate exhale,
the nausea from the fluids
rushing to my head due to lack of gravity.

Could we fly past the edges of the atmosphere
and leave our worries behind?
In search for something greater,
a healing this world let rot
and turn into toxic fungi.

My mother once told me that this was God,
the answer to a black hole,
the one who could froth
our Milky Way out or into existence.

To me this idea had no friction.
I couldn't grasp it,
but somehow Jupiter's gassy surface had handles.
Somehow I believed in a galaxy
that astronomers couldn't measure,
and I prayed to the sun,
and let the lullabies of the moon consume me.

I see now why my dad watches
Lost in Space, The Orville, and Star Trek.
Maybe it's because I can see Mars from my back porch,
or maybe it's James Webb's cluster of galaxies.
The idea of an infinite universe, infinite suns,
an infinite number of times a star can explode
and create a new galaxy worth living in.

NEPTUNE
IV

Neptune is the farthest planet from the sun.

Stolen Vocal Cords

To Anna Marie, the sales rep at the Infiniti car dealership
who I spoke with on the phone
when you accused me of being an intruder,
a thief, an impersonator of my own self.
You weren't the first person to believe my voice
inappropriate for someone who looked like me.
A Black girl with a soothing voice
like John Legend; "We're just ordinary people."

Deep enough to tremble souls with my words,
push people into action with my verbs.
An academic whose vocal strings played sounds
of comfort to professors as university jargonists
massaged their bows across my neck to their liking.

My voice a song composed
of my mother's vocal tenor from church choir,
my older brother's journey into puberty,
my father's notorious lullabies.
At times, one with my emotions
too afraid to raise an octave;
I'd be stuck in my vulnerabilities.
Helpless, like dangling guitar strings cut
for the pleasure of recklessness.

My voice has psychopathic tendencies.
Its inability to empathize with its rightful host
has made it an outcast in a prejudiced society.
It rebels because it seeks the attention and respect
harnessed by the tuba, the trombone.
You see, words like power, courage, strength
are said to be packaged only
in the leftmost keys in a modern piano
As if my voice was stolen from a bearded,
broad-shouldered, hair-receding, middle-aged
being and I am the thief,
the burglar in the middle of the night.

But I am no thief. At least, a bassoon;
too much range to grip.
So heavy you need a harness to control.
Let the vibrato speak to your soul.

The TEAser

Sit,
sip, sonder.
I am taking a moment
of your time.
Let the bourbon settle
on your palate

as earl grazes your soul,
and bergamot brightens
your mood content,
until my sugar caress
reaches your heart.

Let it
be so
intense
and smooth
like apricot's skin.
Let my smoked cinnamon
toast your nostrils.

Your hair standing
straight up
above your spinal cord.
Chills. Barrel sweet.

***Cocktail Recipe:**
The TEAser

Woodford Reserve Bourbon 1.5oz
Earl Grey Rich Syrup 0.25oz
Apricot Syrup 0.25oz
2 Dashes of Angostura Bitters
Smoked Cinnamon after pour

NiiiGahh?

Shut the fuck up
You sooo stooopid
Insults I hear my teenage
students shout loud enough
for everyone in the classroom to hear

A deflection,
A dichotomy,
An axis splitting the plane

I am not like you
stooopid
You should be ashamed
stooopid
How you don't know that
stooopid
You should feel bad
stooopid

You a dumb ass nigga
Ditched class to smoke weed
in the bathroom and got suspended
ass nigga

Dumb ass nigga
Didn't go to school
for a year now don't know fractions
ass nigga

Stupid ass nigga
Lived out of his mama's
van and failed Algebra
ass nigga

They can't always see
that we all stupid ass niggas

She Didn't Really Listen to 80s R&B

so i wrote her a Strawberry Letter;
formulated her some Luther Vandross
I thought she'd remember;
like psychic nostalgia

and took my time with every individual track,
so she could indulge in The Emotions
of a perfectly crafted playlist;
engulfed in pulsating horns, vibrant bass,
and electric guitars

Hoped the melodies of Stevie
wouldn't make her wheezy,
trying to sing every note,
while Marvin gazes through her psyche
with an antidote for the world

Every Gap Band filled with lyrics to kill
the evil in the air with soulful bliss,
and a kiss from Anita; the best that's she's got

Gonna Chaka your fingertips
and trap you in a Maze,
so enticing you'd gladly walk in circles

Zoom past the open Commodores,
and let the fresh air pass you
like you're feeling the pressure
of Earth Wind and Fire all at once

Happy Memorial Day

We celebrate my uncle on Memorial Day
because he was a soldier
who died in a war zone
19 bullets fired like they preyed upon his fate
Torn flesh upon his face like they were welcoming
the light of the heavens with the blood of the lamb
But you were no sacrifice

You were the little boy who fell in love
with playing the drums
The boy who I thought was disgusting
for eating his boogers in preschool
The boy who I moved my tassel to the right with
as we finished our senior year of high school

Now we celebrate your birthday
on an unusual occasion
to remember those lives
who died in the armed forces

But what about the forces
on the streets of East Oakland?
The forces that equipped young
black boys with military weapons?
The forces that burden the very
existence of success for Black futures?
The forces that ended your life just as it began?
The forces that makes Black youth believe
that to have power is to have a gun
and to exert that power is to shoot it?

I'm sorry that no one prepared you;
that there was
no training, no armor
just black hoodie,
black pants, black sneakers
that made you a magnet to silver bullets

I am sorry that I had my whole life
to get to know you better and I abused it
I am sorry that it is so easy for me to forget
the Black bodies that remain nameless
Forgive me or forgive me not
but your name is in my heart
every 25th day of March I will say I love you
for every time that I did not

The Sunken Place

I've fallen for you and you don't even know it.
I had a daydream of you while writing this poem.
That's why it took an hour to finish
and only two minutes to write.

You see, I always knew what I wanted to say,
but sometimes distractions speak
louder than words. You make me feel
like sentences are obsolete.

When I say I have fallen I mean
sunken place fallen. Like I can see myself
outside of myself. Fallen like I've broken my arm
trying to climb a tree but my mind is fixed
on your smile, an adrenaline rush.

I laughed when I realized how much
I have not said in the last 22 lines.
You are a journey I have yet to finish,
inside of another journey I have yet to tell you.

But maybe one day you will see
much better than I can write.

The
Hate
U
Give
Little
Infants
Fucks
Everybody

The meadow sway
so that we
can feast upon it
Get lost in its eyes
Relax upon its
bosom
And cozy up
next to its green
under the sun

Hate casts a shadow
over every dark citizen
a worse always worser
a bad always deadly
a sad always depression

U created this battlefield
filled with sharp razors
Concrete
hot enough to boil
the flesh off the bone

Give us this freedom
that you stole, so my
meadow can sway
So I can have the luxury
of feeling worse not
worser on a deadly day

Little ones be appalled
at the scraps we left
Replace green with
concrete jungles
No small animals left

Infants were rejected
even before a seed
The world is ending
so we don't need

Fucks to give are
always absent minded
Find the truth and
discover what's behind it

Everybody, hurry, come
so that we can feast
we are owed a debt
So we gone eat

A Demisexual Love Story

I've already thought through a future with you
Not in a fairytale way or anything like that
More like an ambitious moth
trying to escape its natural attraction to light
No control

I worked out all the kinks
Imagined the fights we would have
The travel adventures
The awkward meetings with your parents
The deaths and worries that would make us stronger

Not in a romantic way or anything like that
I won't read this at our wedding
More like I'm an unemployed false prophet
Like I have another future in my head and
I have yet to tell you of our overlapping timelines

My love for you is not only
womb-bound, for now,
but hit me like water broken
Foot
Pedal
Gas
hospital
You built a highway over my home and called it yours

Not in a I'm-falling-for-you kind of way or anything like that
More like day 60 you asked if I wanted to hang out with you
My *nice you're really cool* turned into
yes to anything you would ever ask
The plane wheels left the ground
My heart sank
My ears popped

And
I probably like you a lot more than you like me
Not in a let's-make-this-a-date kind of way or anything like that
More like if your ticket is 24D can I be 24E til the plane lands
My connection to you needs time
even though I can probably predict where we'll end up

Next Generation Stargazer

You said, *I'll chop off yo neck*
and spit down yo throat
to a child—your own child

Now your children laugh about it
over Safeway apple juice
and store-bought honey-baked ham
on Thanksgiving
from pain or joy, I can't tell

But I wonder if you were as slick
as my father's father with your words
My aunt once gave me
a framed picture of him
In his smile I still can't see
the terror they speak of

But I could tell that the pitch of their laughter,
the slow exhale of their words,
and the side eye of intention
were a signature of their catharsis

A Bermuda Triangle between three siblings
held memories that you could only get
a glimpse of if you found the moon in their eyes

As terrifying as the Atlantic Slave Trade,
that moon was their northern star
Me, a next generation stargazer

My Brother Got Me a Gold Chain

I was a tomboy in 5th grade.
The style I most aligned with:
oversized jeans, white or black
large t-shirt, snapback with a team on it.

It was armor for the boy who was shot
and killed up the street from our house.
At the time, the only armor I knew
that offered immediate belonging.

I just wanted to play basketball not in a skirt,
wanted to fit in, in a way that said
I could also fall to the ground,
become completely filthy, and not blink an eye—

mostly in anticipation of that rebound:
Box out,
get out of my way,
put back, and
off the backboard.
Yes, you got scored on by a girl!
Lift your head up champ.

◆

Later that year, I decided to get cornrows.
My Nana looked at me.
But not really at me,
at what she'd thought I'd become.
Told me I looked like a boy
and other things I can't remember.
Maybe she was disappointed.

In 6th grade, I never wore pants
that didn't fit tight,
or hats of any kind,
or oversized t-shirts.
Maybe I found new armor,
maybe I was finding myself,
maybe disappointment was
enough to keep me in a shell.

Years later, my brother bought
me a gold chain for Christmas;
a missing object in a time capsule
buried by a 10-year-old me.

Resistance Song

After Bob Marley
"Redemption Song"

Will our stories be sold? Or
will our souls live forever?
Screaming war has just begun
This war has bore a son
Soldiers, beating hearts, guns
We, swallowed whole by the graveyards
Come home again these bullets aren't our
sovereignty

Help me sing this song
of liberation
All I ever wanted
Resistance songs
Resistance songs

Be forever unyoked from hegemony, we
beholder of our conscious minds
Don't allow coppers to define us
They won't control our destinies
Some say we are one in the same,
killing out of fear, scared of free
We don't need to hide from the truth
Assemble! The fight is here

Help me sing this song
of liberation
All I ever wanted
Resistance songs
Resistance songs
Resistance songs

Be forever unyoked from hegemony, we
beholder of our conscious minds
Don't allow coppers to define us
They won't control our destinies
Some say we are one in the same,
killing out of fear, scared of free
We don't need to hide from the truth
Assemble! The fight is here
Help me sing this song
of liberation
All I ever wanted
Resistance songs
I ever wanted
Resistance songs
of liberation
Liberation

Hear a snippet of the song.
Sung by the author and
guitar by Maricela

Words I Told Myself Before Writing This Book

Thank you for being my northern star:
a launching point I have yet to find
hidden somewhere in places of books
places of memories that have yet to be mine.

There's a sense though that I'll abandon my path
and the ball of light I am chasing will shatter.
The pieces, I will neglect putting back together,
deem pointless for chasing after every little one.

I keep this fear in my pocket as a reminder
of an oncoming disaster. A reminder that I am
not always in control. A reminder that the fire
may spread and life will keep going as if unaware
of its ultimate demise. A reminder that anything big
enough can seem small and anything small enough
can seem big so I guess I'm starting small,
waiting to shine as bright as the sun

ACKNOWLEDGEMENTS

You already know that it took a village to put this one together. It starts with my parents of course. You gave me so much more than I could have ever asked. You are one of the reasons that I survived and lived. Your love and support means the world. I hope that you see this as our accomplishment. I love you. To Correna, thank you for showing me how to be unapologetic and bold. I appreciate your love and advice always. To Nana, thank you for always saying it like it is and never letting me go home empty handed. Your care is heaven sent. To Alex and Amara, thank you for living in your truth. You encourage me to do the same and I will always love y'all for that.

To my friends, thank you for your love and support. Princess, thank you for being one of the first to read my book and tell me your thoughts. I appreciate your friendship more than you know. Maricela, thank you for helping me find the music in myself and for being an amazing musician. I appreciate you and love you very much.

To Nancy, thank you for allowing me to experience a love so sacred and allowing me to become a love poet.

To the ones responsible for helping this book come into fruition: I am forever grateful to Hiram, Emily, Laura, Amy and the Community Literature Initiative program for giving me the space and tools to make this happen. Thanks Paula for completing the astronaut art. Thank you to the CLI season 10 USC chapter for all of your feedback and support. I have grown so much from your words and efforts and I appreciate the time I was able to learn from you all.

NOTES

*Foxy Shirley and The TEAser are both poems about cocktails also created by the author. Learn more @spokensip.

ABOUT THE AUTHOR

Tichina was born and raised in Oakland, California and is now a math and computer science teacher in South LA, mixologist, and poet searching the universe for infinite inspiration. She currently resides in Inglewood, California.